ENRIQUE TRUJILLO

Conquer the Sales Game

Expert Training for Direct Sales Agents

First edition

ISBN: 978-1-962133-45-6

Editing by Elanor Harris

This book was professionally typeset on Reedsy.
Find out more at reedsy.com

Contents

Acknowledgement

I would like to express my sincere appreciation to
Elanor Harris
for her expertise and dedication,
which significantly enhanced the quality of this manuscript.
She provided invaluable insights, meticulous editing, and unwavering
support throughout this process.
Her keen eye for detail and commitment to clarity
have undoubtedly played a crucial role in shaping this work.
I am genuinely grateful for the opportunity to collaborate with someone of
her caliber. Thank you, Elanor Harris,
Thank you for your tireless efforts and for bringing this project to fruition.
Your contributions have made a lasting impact,
and I am grateful for your hard work.
Elanor Harris is an academic copy editor based in Liverpool, UK.
ejhproofreading@gmail.com

To Matt Rudnitsky and his crew at *Platypus Publishing*
with their continuous motivation to make this happen, inspired by his
excellence in writing, and the sheer determination of other fabulous authors
who have
also provided much encouragement and support.

1

Introduction to Direct Sales

The Importance of DSAs

I n the dynamic and ever-evolving world of sales, DSAs play a crucial role. These individuals are the backbone of any successful sales team, as they are the ones who directly interact with customers, build relationships, and ultimately close deals. This subchapter highlights the significance of DSAs in the sales industry and emphasizes the need for continuous training and development in this niche.

DSAs are the face of the company they represent. They are the first point of contact for potential customers and are responsible for creating a positive impression. Their ability to effectively communicate a product's or service's benefits is crucial in influencing customers' buying decisions.

A well-trained DSA possesses the skills to understand customers' needs, address their concerns, and provide tailored solutions. Their expertise and knowledge instill confidence in customers, leading to increased sales and customer loyalty.

Sales training is of paramount importance for DSAs. It equips them with the necessary tools and techniques to excel. Continuous training ensures that agents are updated with industry trends, sales strategies, and product knowledge. It helps them adapt to changing customer preferences and market dynamics. Moreover, training enhances their communication and negotiation skills, enabling them to handle objections and close deals more effectively.

DSAs have a unique advantage over other sales channels. Their ability to establish personal connections with customers fosters trust and loyalty. By understanding customers more deeply, they can provide personalized recommendations and solutions, creating a memorable buying experience. This personalized approach increases customer satisfaction and encourages referrals and repeat business.

Furthermore, DSAs act as brand ambassadors for the company they represent. They embody the company's values, mission, and culture, and their interactions shape the customers' perception of the brand. A well-trained and professional DSA can significantly enhance the brand image, increasing credibility and market share.

In conclusion, DSAs are indispensable in the sales industry. Their role as the face of the company, their ability to build relationships, and their personalized approach to selling make them invaluable assets. Continuous training and development are essential to equip DSAs with the skills needed to excel in their role. By investing in sales training, companies can empower their DSAs to conquer the sales game and achieve remarkable success in the competitive market.

A high mark for any DSA is to be a brand ambassador.

For example, Oprah's genuine and authentic approach resonates with her audience, making her an effective ambassador for products or services. Her endorsement goes beyond traditional advertising and directly influences consumer trust and confidence. This example can underscore the importance of strong and relatable brand ambassadors, particularly in direct sales, where personal connections play a crucial role.

Oprah Winfrey has been an influential figure and a powerful brand ambassador for various products and initiatives throughout her career. She can connect with people personally, and her endorsement has significantly impacted sales.

As a representative in the San Francisco office for *Peach Tree Bancard*, in 1990, my first task was to achieve excellence in the office and become a top agent. This came as a contest where the top salesperson would receive a beautiful gold company logo, with a minimum of 20 monthly accounts to qualify. So, I did that and became the top sales leader that month.

Bill Klein, a regional manager assigned to the Walnut Creek office, could not continue the following month, so they needed a replacement. I was offered the sales director position, and this event started my journey as a "Brand ambassador."

Understanding the Sales Game

In the world of sales, success doesn't come quickly. It takes skill, knowledge, and a deep understanding of the sales game. This subchapter aims to provide DSAs with a comprehensive understanding of the sales process and equip them with the necessary tools to excel in their profession.

The first step to conquering the sales game is understanding the importance of sales training. Sales training is the backbone of every successful salesperson. It equips them with the knowledge and skills to build relationships, identify customer needs, and close deals. This subchapter will delve into various aspects of sales training, including effective communication techniques, objection-handling strategies, and negotiation skills.

One crucial aspect of understanding the sales game is recognizing the importance of building strong relationships with customers. DSAs must focus on establishing trust and rapport with their clients, as this lays the foundation for successful sales. This subchapter will provide valuable insights on building and maintaining customer relationships, including tips for effective networking, follow-up techniques, and personalized customer service.

Another key aspect of the sales game is identifying customer needs. DSAs must understand what drives their customers, pain points, and desires. By understanding a prospect's needs, sales agents can tailor their pitch and offer solutions that resonate with clients. This subchapter will explore various strategies for identifying customer needs, including active listening, asking the right questions, and conducting a thorough needs analysis.

Setting up Properly

To establish rapport, the University of California did a study where they found that 40% accounts for physiology, 35% is voice inflection, and 25% are words.
 To set up your presentation properly, you will need to:

1. Establish rapport
2. Find the need
3. Sell the idea

Once you can ask questions and find an area where your product or service can fill the need, it's important to sell the idea that your product or service is the right solution.
 Identifying customers' needs is an important skill to develop. This is done primarily via observation and asking the right questions. Once rapport has been established, you can ask questions to find the need.

Asking Questions

Ask the right questions.

Try to identify their most essential needs.

Sales Representative: "I'm glad we've had a chance to connect, and I appreciate you sharing more about your business so far. To better understand your needs, could you tell me more about the key goals or challenges your company currently faces in [relevant area, e.g., marketing, operations, efficiency]?"

Prospect: "Sure, one of our main challenges is [specific challenge]."

Sales Representative: "Thank you for sharing that. We need to tailor our solutions to meet your unique challenges. Can you elaborate on how [specific challenge] impacts your day-to-day operations or overall business objectives?"

This approach allows the sales representative to delve deeper into the prospect's specific pain points, opening the door for a more detailed discussion about how the offered product or service can address those challenges effectively. It demonstrates a genuine interest in understanding the prospect's business and sets the stage for a more personalized sales presentation.

Every salesperson's ultimate goal is closing the deal. However, closing can be a daunting task for many DSAs. This subchapter will provide valuable insights into effective closing techniques, such as creating a sense of urgency, handling objections, and overcoming common sales barriers. Additionally, it will cover the importance of follow-up and post-sales service in building long-term customer relationships.

In conclusion, mastering the sales game is crucial for DSAs looking to excel in their profession. This subchapter provides a comprehensive overview of the critical elements of the sales process, including sales training, relationship-building, identifying customer needs, and closing deals. By understanding and implementing these strategies, DSAs can conquer the sales game and achieve unparalleled career success.

Sales based on the Law of Averages

Advancing your sales career will involve understanding and improving your law of averages.

The most important aspect involves the number of prospects you visit in person or over the phone. Besides improving your number of prospects and presentations, your quality of delivery is where most improvement occurs. In addition, the following factors must be considered.

1. Diverse Needs and Preferences: Each prospect has unique needs, preferences, and decision-making criteria. Not every presentation will align perfectly with what a particular prospect is looking for, leading to variations in buying decisions.
2. Timing and Readiness: Prospects may not be ready to purchase during the presentation. Factors such as budget cycles, internal decision-making processes, or external market conditions can influence the timing of a buying decision.
3. Objections and Concerns: Some prospects may have objections or concerns not adequately addressed during the presentation. Overcoming objections and building trust are crucial aspects of the sales process, and these factors can affect whether a prospect decides to buy.
4. Competitive Landscape: In many industries, there's often competition. Even if your presentation is strong, prospects may be considering alternatives. The competitive landscape can impact the conversion rate

as prospects weigh different options.

5. Budget Constraints: Budget considerations play a significant role. Even if prospects are interested, they may not have the financial resources to purchase at a particular time. Budget constraints can delay or prevent a sale.

6. Follow-up and Relationship Building: The sales process doesn't end with the initial presentation. Effective follow-up and ongoing relationship-building are essential. Some prospects may require additional interactions and nurturing before they are ready to commit to a purchase.

7. Decision-Making Structure: In B2B sales, the decision-making process often involves multiple stakeholders. Aligning the interests and priorities of various decision-makers can be complex, impacting the conversion rate.

Understanding these factors helps sales professionals refine their strategies, improve presentations, and adapt their approach to addressing different prospects' needs and concerns. It also emphasizes the importance of a systematic and strategic sales process to maximize the likelihood of successful conversions.

I had a severe commission cut during my first weeks as a new sales director in Walnut Creek, CA. Still, a few months into it, I eventually led that office to become the #1 regional office in the US out of 100 other regional offices, including New York, San Francisco, and Los Angeles.

Common Challenges in Direct Sales

Direct sales can be a rewarding and lucrative career, but it also comes with its fair share of challenges. As a DSA, you must be prepared to overcome these obstacles to succeed in the competitive sales world. In this subchapter, we will explore some of the most common challenges faced by DSAs and provide expert advice on how to conquer them.

One of the biggest challenges in direct sales is rejection. It is not uncommon for sales agents to face rejection daily. Whether a potential customer declines your offer or a prospect ignores your follow-up calls, rejection can affect your confidence and motivation. However, it's important to remember that rejection is not personal. Instead of dwelling on the negative, use it as an opportunity to learn and improve. Develop a mindset that views rejection as a stepping stone towards success.

Another challenge in direct sales is building a solid customer base. Acquiring new customers can be time-consuming and requires consistent effort. It is essential to identify your target audience and develop strategies to attract and retain them. Building customer relationships through personalized communication and exceptional customer service can help create a loyal customer base.

Time management is also a common challenge for DSAs. Balancing prospecting, follow-ups, presentations, and administrative tasks can be overwhelming. To overcome this challenge, prioritize your tasks and create a schedule that allows you to focus on high-value activities. Use technology and automation tools to streamline your processes and maximize your productivity.

Effective Time Management

Time management is crucial for sales professionals to maximize productivity and achieve their goals. Here are some great tools and techniques to help salespeople use their time more effectively.

1. Calendar and Scheduling Tools
   Google Calendar, Microsoft Outlook: Use calendar tools to schedule and

organize meetings, calls, and follow-ups. Set reminders to stay on top of important tasks.

2. Task Management Tools
   Trello, Asana, or Todoist: These tools help you organize tasks, set priorities, and track progress. They also help you manage daily to-do lists and ensure nothing falls through the cracks.

3. Customer Relationship Management (CRM) Systems
   Salesforce, HubSpot, or Zoho CRM: CRM systems help organize customer information, track interactions, and manage leads. They streamline the sales process and provide insights for better decision-making.

4. Email Productivity Tools
   Boomerang, SaneBox: These tools help manage emails efficiently, schedule emails for later, and prioritize important messages. They can reduce inbox clutter and improve responsiveness.

5. Sales Engagement Platforms
   Outreach, SalesLoft: These platforms automate and streamline sales outreach, including email sequences and follow-ups. They can save time and improve the consistency of communication.

6. Automation Tools
   Zapier, Integromat: Automate repetitive tasks and integrate different applications. For example, automate lead data entry from forms to your CRM.

7. Time Blocking
   Allocate specific blocks of time for different activities, such as prospecting, meetings, and administrative tasks. This helps maintain focus and prevents multitasking.

8. Prioritization Techniques

Eisenhower Matrix: Prioritize tasks based on urgency and importance. Focus on high-priority tasks that align with your sales goals.

9. Batch Processing

Group similar tasks together and tackle them during dedicated time blocks. This reduces context-switching and improves overall efficiency.

10. Set Clear Goals and Objectives

Define specific, measurable, and achievable goals. Having a clear direction helps prioritize tasks that contribute to those goals.

11. Regular Reviews and Reflection

Take time at the end of the day or week to review accomplishments, assess what worked well, and identify areas for improvement.

12. Continuous Learning

Stay updated on industry trends, sales techniques, and tools. Investing time in learning can lead to more effective strategies and tactics.

By combining these tools and techniques, sales professionals can enhance their time management skills, reduce manual workload, and focus on activities that drive meaningful results in their sales efforts.

Additionally, staying motivated and resilient in the face of obstacles is crucial for success in direct sales. It's easy to get discouraged when facing rejection or experiencing slow sales periods. Surround yourself with a supportive network of fellow sales agents who can provide guidance and encouragement. Continuously invest in your personal development through sales training programs and books to stay motivated and improve your skills.

In conclusion, DSAs face several challenges in their profession. By adopting a positive mindset, developing effective strategies, managing time efficiently, and staying motivated, you can conquer these challenges and succeed in the sales game. Remember, every challenge is an opportunity for growth and learning. With determination and perseverance, you can overcome any obstacle that comes your way and excel in your direct sales career.

2

Building a Strong Foundation

Developing a Growth Mindset

I n direct sales, success is not just about having a charming personality or a persuasive pitch. It is about having the right mindset – a growth mindset. A *growth mindset* is the key to unlocking your full potential and achieving extraordinary results in the sales game.

So, what exactly is a growth mindset? Simply put, it is the belief that your abilities and intelligence can be developed through dedication and hard work. It is the understanding that failure is not the end but a stepping stone to learning and improvement.

DSAs with a growth mindset approach every challenge as an opportunity for growth. They embrace failure as a learning experience, using it to analyze what went wrong and how they can do better next time. Instead of being discouraged, they see setbacks as a chance to develop new strategies and refine their skills.

Adopting a positive attitude is one of the first steps towards developing a growth mindset. Believe in your ability to learn and improve, no matter the circumstances. Surround yourself with positive influences, whether through books, podcasts, or mentors who inspire and push you to reach new heights.

It is also crucial to set realistic goals and constantly strive for self-improvement. DSAs with a growth mindset are never satisfied with mediocrity. They constantly seek out new knowledge, attend training sessions, and engage in self-reflection to identify areas for improvement.

Strive to Improve

Improving sales skills, including voice inflection, body language, and other aspects, can significantly enhance a salesperson's effectiveness. Here are examples and tips for developing these skills:

1. Voice Inflection

Practice Tone Variation: Experiment with different tones to convey enthusiasm, confidence, and empathy. Use a warm, engaging tone during positive points and a more serious tone for essential details.

Record and Review: Record your sales calls or presentations. Listen to how you sound and identify areas for improvement. Pay attention to pacing, emphasis, and modulation.

2. Body Language

Maintain Eye Contact: Establishing and maintaining eye contact conveys confidence and sincerity. It shows that you are engaged and attentive.

Open Posture: Stand or sit with an open and relaxed posture. Avoid crossing arms, as it may signal defensiveness. Open body language fosters trust.

3. Active Listening

Reflective Listening: Repeat or paraphrase the prospect's words to demonstrate understanding. This shows that you are actively engaged in the conversation.

Non-Verbal Cues: Use nodding and other non-verbal cues to signal you are listening. Avoid interrupting and give the prospect space to express themselves.

4. Empathy

Put Yourself in Their Shoes: Try to understand the prospect's perspective and challenges. Show empathy by acknowledging their concerns and expressing a genuine desire to help.

Use Empathetic Language: Incorporate phrases like "I understand how that can be challenging" to convey empathy without sounding insincere.

5. Adaptability

Tailor Your Approach: Recognize and adapt to the prospect's communication style. If they prefer concise information, avoid lengthy explanations. If they appreciate details, provide more in-depth insights.

6. Confidence

Preparation: Thoroughly prepare for meetings and presentations. Knowing your product, industry, and prospect's needs boosts confidence.

Positive Self-Talk: Replace negative thoughts with positive affirmations. Confidence is reflected in both verbal and non-verbal communication.

7. Storytelling

Create Engaging Narratives: Develop compelling stories that highlight the benefits of your product or service. Storytelling captivates the prospect's attention and makes your message memorable.

8. Closing Techniques

Trial Closes: Throughout the conversation, use trial closes to gauge the prospect's interest. For example, "How does this solution sound to you?" Adjust your approach based on their responses.

Assumptive Close: Assume the prospect is ready to move forward and discuss the next steps. For instance, "When would be a good time for our implementation team to start?"

9. Continuous Learning

Training Programs: Attend sales training programs, workshops, or online courses. Stay updated on industry best practices and continuously refine your skills.

10. Feedback and Coaching

Seek Feedback: Ask colleagues or mentors for feedback on your sales pitches or presentations. Constructive criticism is valuable for improvement.

Role-Playing: Practice scenarios with a colleague or mentor through role-playing. This helps refine your skills in a controlled environment.

By consistently practicing and incorporating these examples into your sales approach, you can enhance your overall sales skills and build stronger connections with prospects. Remember that improvement is ongoing, and feedback is crucial in refining your techniques.

Furthermore, developing resilience is a critical component of a growth mindset. In the world of sales, rejection is inevitable. However, instead of taking rejection personally, embrace it as a challenge to overcome. Learn from each rejection, adapt your approach, and keep pushing forward.

Lastly, surround yourself with a supportive network of like-minded individuals. Connect with other DSAs who share your passion for growth and success. Share ideas, exchange experiences, and provide support to one another. Together, you can create an environment that fosters growth and propels everyone towards achieving their goals.

In conclusion, developing a growth mindset is crucial for DSAs who want to conquer the sales game. Embrace failure as an opportunity to learn and improve. Adopt a positive attitude, set realistic goals, and constantly seek self-improvement. Build resilience and surround yourself with a supportive network. With a *growth mindset*, you have the power to achieve extraordinary results and become a sales superstar.

Setting Realistic Goals

Success in direct sales is often measured by achieving sales goals. However, setting unrealistic goals can lead to frustration, demotivation, and failure. As a DSA, it is crucial to understand the importance of setting realistic goals and how to do so.

One of the first steps in setting realistic goals is clearly understanding your capabilities and limitations. Assess your skills, knowledge, and experience to determine what is achievable within a given timeframe. By setting goals that align with your abilities, you set yourself up for success and avoid unnecessary disappointment.

Another critical aspect of setting realistic goals is being specific and measurable. Instead of setting a vague goal like "increase sales," set a specific target such as "increase sales by 10% in the next quarter." This allows you to track your progress and make necessary adjustments.

It is also important to consider external factors impacting your ability to achieve your goals. Consider market trends, competition, and other relevant factors influencing your sales performance. By acknowledging these factors, you can set goals that are not only realistic but also adaptable.

In addition to being specific and measurable, goals should also be time-bound. Set a deadline for achieving your weekly, monthly, or quarterly goals. This creates urgency and helps you stay focused and motivated to reach your objectives.

Furthermore, breaking down larger goals into smaller, manageable tasks is essential. By dividing your goals into smaller milestones, you can track your progress more effectively and celebrate small victories. This approach also makes your goals less overwhelming and more attainable.

Lastly, regularly review and reassess your goals. As you gain experience and knowledge, your goals may need to be adjusted. Set aside time to reflect on your progress, analyze what is working and what isn't, and make necessary changes to your goals and strategies.

Remember, setting realistic goals is not about limiting your potential but ensuring that you set yourself up for success. By being specific, measurable, time-bound, and adaptable, you can conquer the sales game and achieve remarkable results as a DSA.

Creating a Personal Development Plan

Continuous growth and development are vital for success in the highly competitive world of direct sales. As a DSA, investing time and effort in your personal development is crucial to stay ahead of the game. A well-crafted personal development plan can provide the tools and strategies to conquer the sales game.

A personal development plan serves as a roadmap for achieving your goals and maximizing your potential as a DSA. It helps you identify your strengths and weaknesses, set realistic targets, and outline the steps needed to reach those goals. Here are some key elements to consider when creating your personal development plan:

1. Self-Assessment: Begin by assessing your current skills, knowledge, and abilities. Evaluate your strengths and weaknesses in various areas, such as communication, negotiation, product knowledge, and relationship building. This self-assessment will clearly understand where you stand and where you need to improve.

2. Set Clear Goals: Define your short-term and long-term goals. These goals should be specific, measurable, achievable, relevant, and time-bound (SMART). Clearly articulate what you want to achieve, whether it's increasing your sales volume by a certain percentage or expanding your client base.

3. Identify Development Areas: Based on your self-assessment and goals, pinpoint the areas that require improvement. These could be enhancing your product knowledge, mastering new sales techniques, improving your time management skills, or enhancing your emotional intelligence. Prioritize these areas according to their importance and relevance to your goals.

4. Learning Opportunities: Research and explore various learning opportunities that align with your development areas. These could include attending workshops, seminars, webinars, or enrolling in online courses. Take advantage of resources offered by your company, industry associations, or reputable sales training programs. Additionally, consider seeking a mentor within the industry who can provide guidance and support.

5. Implementation and Review: Once you have identified the learning opportunities, create an action plan to implement your development activities. Break down the plan into smaller, achievable tasks and set deadlines for completion. Regularly review your progress and make adjustments as needed.

Remember, personal development is an ongoing process. Continuously seek ways to improve and stay updated on the latest sales techniques, industry trends, and customer preferences. Regularly revisit and update your personal development plan to remain relevant and aligned with your evolving goals.

Creating and following a well-structured personal development plan will enhance your skills and knowledge and gain a competitive edge in the dynamic world of direct sales. Embrace personal growth as a lifelong journey and let it propel you to conquer the sales game.

3

Mastering Effective Communication

Active Listening Skills

Success in direct sales hinges on effective communication and building strong relationships with clients. One crucial aspect of communication that often gets overlooked is active listening. As a DSA, mastering active listening skills can significantly impact your sales performance and overall success in the field.

Active listening involves hearing your prospects' words and understanding their needs, concerns, and motivations. By listening attentively to your potential customers, you can effectively tailor your pitch to address their pain points. Remember, effective communication is a two-way street; actively listening shows your prospects that you genuinely care about their needs. By honing this skill, you can uncover valuable insights, gain trust, and establish rapport with your clients.

To become an active listener, start by eliminating distractions and focusing solely on the conversation. Put away your mobile phone, shut down your computer, and make eye contact with your client. This will convey your undivided attention and show them you value their time and input.

Another crucial aspect of active listening is asking open-ended questions. Doing so encourages your clients to provide detailed responses, allowing you to understand their needs and preferences better. Open-ended questions also demonstrate your genuine interest in their thoughts and opinions, fostering a sense of trust and rapport.

Open-ended questions are a great way to engage with potential customers and gather valuable information. Here are examples for both establishing rapport and during a presentation for a (DSA):

Here are examples of some open-ended questions to establish rapport, engage your prospects, and gain valuable information.

1. **Personal Interests**
    - "What are some of your hobbies or interests outside of work?"
    - "Tell me about a recent accomplishment you're proud of."

2. **Experience with Products/Services**
    - "Have you used similar products/services in the past? What was your experience like?"
    - "How did you first hear about our company?"

3. **Goals and Challenges**
    - "What goals do you have for [relevant period] that we could help you with?"
    - "Are there any specific challenges you currently face in [relevant area]?"

During a Presentation, try this:

1. **Needs and Preferences**
    - "Can you share more about what features are most important to you in

[product/service]?"
   - "How do you envision using [product/service] daily?"

2. Decision-Making Process
   - "What factors are most important to you when deciding?"
   - "How involved are others in your decision-making process?"

3. Customization
   - "Are there specific aspects of [product/service] that you would like to customize to suit your needs better?"
   - "What would an ideal solution look like for you?"

4. Timeline
   - "Do you have a specific timeline for implementing [product/service]?"
   - "How soon would you like to see results or benefits from [product/service]?"

5. Feedback and Concerns
   - "What are your initial thoughts or concerns about what I've presented so far?"
   - "Is there anything you'd like more information on or clarification about?"

Remember, the goal of open-ended questions is to encourage a detailed and thoughtful response, fostering a deeper conversation and understanding of the customer's needs and preferences.

Paraphrasing and summarizing your clients' words is another effective active listening technique. By repeating their words back to them, you show that you are actively listening and allow them to clarify or expand on their thoughts. This ensures that you have a clear understanding of their needs and prevents any miscommunication.

Non-verbal cues also play a significant role in active listening. Maintain an open and welcoming body language, nod your head to show understanding, and provide appropriate facial expressions to demonstrate your engagement and empathy.

By developing active listening skills, you can identify your client's pain points, offer tailored solutions, and ultimately close more sales. Remember, direct sales are not just about selling a product or service – it's about building meaningful relationships with your clients. Active listening is the key to unlocking those relationships and becoming a trusted advisor in your niche.

In conclusion, mastering active listening skills is crucial to your success as a DSA. You can become an exceptional active listener by eliminating distractions, asking open-ended questions, paraphrasing, and utilizing nonverbal cues. This will strengthen your client relationships and increase your sales effectiveness. So, prioritize active listening in your sales training and watch your results soar.

Effective Verbal Communication

Effective verbal communication is crucial in the fast-paced sales world that can make or break a deal. As a DSA, your ability to convey your message persuasively and confidently can significantly impact your success in the field. This subchapter will provide essential tips and strategies to enhance your verbal communication skills and help you conquer the sales game.

As mentioned earlier, active listening is fundamental.

Next, the power of language cannot be underestimated. The words you choose and how you deliver them can significantly influence the outcome of a sales conversation. Avoid using vague or technical jargon that may confuse your prospects. Instead, use clear and concise language that resonates with them.

Additionally, be mindful of your tone of voice and body language. Projecting confidence, enthusiasm, and empathy can create a positive impression and build rapport with your prospects.

Furthermore, effective verbal communication involves asking the right questions. You demonstrate your willingness to understand and meet their expectations by asking probing questions. Additionally, be prepared to answer objections and concerns confidently. Anticipate potential objections and practice your responses to ensure you can address them smoothly and convincingly.

Lastly, practice, practice, practice! Verbal communication is a skill that can be honed through consistent practice. Role-play scenarios and simulate sales conversations with colleagues or mentors to refine communication techniques. Pay attention to your strengths and areas for improvement, and actively seek feedback to continuously enhance your verbal communication skills.

In conclusion, effective verbal communication is a vital asset for DSAs. By actively listening, choosing the correct language, asking the right questions, and practicing consistently, you can become a master communicator and conquer the sales game. Remember, every sales conversation is an opportunity to connect with your prospects, build relationships, and close deals. With these strategies in your toolkit, you are on your way to achieving sales excellence.

Non-verbal communication and Body Language

While verbal communication plays a significant role, non-verbal cues and body language often make a difference in building rapport, establishing trust, and closing deals. This subchapter will delve into the importance of non-verbal communication and body language for DSAs, providing valuable insights and techniques to enhance their sales game.

DSAs constantly interact with potential clients, and their ability to read and interpret non-verbal cues can give them a significant advantage. Understanding body language can help agents gauge their prospects' level of interest, comfort, and engagement. By paying attention to subtle cues such as facial expressions, gestures, and posture, agents can adapt their approach to better connect with their audience.

One crucial aspect of non-verbal communication is mirroring or matching the prospect's body language. Mirroring creates a sense of familiarity and trust, making the prospect more receptive to the agent's message. However, it is essential to maintain authenticity and avoid becoming too obvious or intrusive in the mirroring process.

Another valuable technique is to observe micro-expressions, which are brief facial expressions that reveal genuine emotions. By honing their ability to recognize these subtle changes, DSAs can better understand the needs and desires of their prospects. This insight allows agents to tailor their pitch and address concerns more effectively, ultimately increasing their chances of closing the sale.

Furthermore, agents can use body language to convey confidence, credibility, and enthusiasm. Maintaining an open posture, eye contact, and using appropriate hand gestures can enhance the agent's presence and command attention. Conversely, agents must be aware of negative body language signals, such as crossed arms or avoiding eye contact, as these can create barriers and hinder effective communication.

This subchapter, DSAs will learn practical exercises and techniques to improve their non-verbal communication skills. By mastering the art of body language, agents will become more persuasive and deepen their understanding of their prospects' needs and motivations. These skills will enable agents to forge stronger connections, overcome objections, and ultimately conquer the sales game.

In conclusion, non-verbal communication and body language are indispensable tools for DSAs. By honing their ability to read and utilize these cues effectively, agents can establish trust, build rapport, and increase their success in closing sales. This subchapter will equip agents with the knowledge and techniques they need to excel in their sales training, setting them apart as expert communicators in the dynamic world of direct sales.

4

Understanding the Sales Process

Prospecting and Lead Generation

P rospecting and lead generation are the lifeblood of success in the ever-evolving sales world. As a DSA, your ability to effectively identify and connect with potential customers is paramount. This subchapter will equip you with the necessary strategies and techniques to conquer the art of prospecting and lead generation, ensuring a steady stream of qualified leads and increased sales.

Prospecting is the initial stage of the sales process, where you actively seek out individuals or businesses who may need your product or service. It involves researching, identifying, and qualifying potential leads, laying the foundation for a successful sales approach.

One of the most effective prospecting techniques is leveraging your existing network. Contact friends, family, and acquaintances, and ask for referrals. People are likelier to trust a recommendation from someone they know and respect, making these leads invaluable. Additionally, utilize social media platforms to expand your network and connect with individuals who align with your target market.

Another powerful strategy is utilizing lead generation tools and technologies. Utilize customer relationship management (CRM) software to track and manage leads efficiently. This helps you stay organized and provides valuable insights into customer behaviors and preferences, enabling you to tailor your approach for maximum impact.

Furthermore, embracing content marketing can significantly boost your lead-generation efforts. Create compelling and informative content, such as blog posts, videos, or infographics, that addresses your target audience's pain points and challenges. By providing value upfront, you establish yourself as an industry expert and build trust with potential leads.

Establishing a consistent and disciplined routine is crucial to maximize your prospecting efforts. Dedicate specific time blocks each day or week solely for prospecting activities. This ensures that you consistently generate new leads and maintain a steady pipeline.

Remember, prospecting and lead generation are ongoing processes. Continuously refine your approach, test new strategies, and adapt to changing market conditions. By mastering the art of prospecting and lead generation, you position yourself as a sales professional who is always one step ahead, ready to conquer the sales game.

In conclusion, prospecting and lead generation are fundamental to the success of DSAs. By implementing the strategies and techniques outlined in this subchapter, you will be equipped to effectively identify and connect with potential customers, ensuring a steady stream of qualified leads and increased sales. Stay proactive, be persistent, and watch as your prospecting efforts pave the way for a successful sales career.

Qualifying Leads

In direct sales, the success of your business relies heavily on your ability to identify and qualify leads. A lead is a potential customer interested in your product or service. However, not all leads are created equal, and DSAs must be able to distinguish between high-quality leads that are likely to convert into sales and those that may not be worth pursuing.

The process of qualifying leads involves gathering information and evaluating the potential of each lead. This step is essential because it allows you to focus your efforts on prospects who are most likely to make a purchase, saving you time and energy in the long run. By effectively qualifying leads, you can increase conversion rates and boost sales.

One of the first steps in qualifying leads is identifying critical criteria indicating a prospect's potential interest. This can include factors such as their budget, need for your product or service, and timeline for purchasing. By asking the right questions and actively listening to their responses, you can gain valuable insights into their interest level and ability to make a buying decision.

Another important aspect of qualifying leads is understanding their buying behavior. This involves analyzing their past purchasing habits, researching their industry, and identifying any pain points they may have. Doing so allows you to tailor your sales approach to their needs and position your product or service as the ideal solution.

Furthermore, qualifying leads requires ongoing communication and follow-up. It is essential to nurture relationships with potential customers, providing them with relevant information and addressing any concerns they may have. By staying engaged and building trust, you increase the likelihood of converting leads into loyal customers.

In conclusion, qualifying leads is crucial for DSAs to maximize their sales potential. Agents can increase conversion rates and achieve sales targets by effectively identifying high-quality leads, understanding their needs, and nurturing relationships. So, take the time to learn and refine your lead qualification techniques, and you will conquer the sales game!

Presenting and Demonstrating Products or Services

In sales, one of the most crucial steps in closing a deal is effectively presenting and demonstrating products or services to potential customers. This subchapter will provide DSAs with expert training on mastering the art of presenting and demonstrating their offerings to increase their sales success.

DSAs need to understand the products or services they are selling thoroughly. This includes knowing the features, benefits, and unique selling points of each offering. With a deep knowledge of what they are selling, agents can confidently and persuasively present their products or services to potential customers.

Next, DSAs must tailor their presentations to their customers' needs and preferences. This requires active listening and asking relevant questions to gather information about the customer's pain points and desires. By customizing the presentation to address these specific needs, agents can strengthen their connection with their audience and demonstrate how their offerings can solve their problems or fulfill their desires.

Visual aids and demonstrations play a vital role in capturing the attention and interest of potential customers. DSAs should incorporate compelling visuals, such as product samples, demonstrations, or testimonials, to make their presentations more engaging and persuasive. This allows customers to see and experience the value of the products or services firsthand, making it easier for them to purchase.

Furthermore, storytelling can be a powerful tool to connect emotionally with customers during the presentation. By sharing relatable stories or case studies of satisfied customers who have benefited from the products or services, agents can tap into the potential customers' emotions and build trust and credibility. This storytelling approach helps customers envision themselves enjoying the same benefits and encourages them to take action.

Lastly, DSAs should always be prepared to handle objections or concerns that may arise during the presentation. Agents can confidently address any doubts or hesitations by anticipating common objections and having well-crafted responses ready, ultimately increasing the chances of closing the sale.

In conclusion, mastering the art of presenting and demonstrating products or services is crucial for DSAs. Agents can significantly enhance their sales success by understanding their offerings, customizing their presentations, incorporating visuals and demonstrations, utilizing storytelling techniques, and effectively handling objections. Continued practice and refinement of these techniques will ultimately lead to increased customer engagement, higher conversion rates, and more sales.

5

Effective Sales Techniques

Building Rapport and Trust

Building rapport and trust with potential customers is crucial for success in direct sales. As a DSA, your ability to establish a connection and gain the trust of your prospects can make or break a sale. This subchapter will explore practical strategies to help you build rapport and trust with your customers.

First and foremost, it is essential to approach every interaction with a genuine and positive attitude. People can sense insincerity, so it is vital to be authentic in your approach. Show a genuine interest in your customers and their needs. Take the time to listen actively and empathize with their concerns. By showing that you genuinely care, you can build a strong foundation of trust.

Another critical aspect of building rapport is finding common ground with your prospects. Look for shared interests or experiences that you can connect on. This can help create a sense of familiarity and build trust. Additionally, be mindful of your body language and non-verbal cues. Maintain eye contact, smile, and use open and welcoming gestures. These simple actions can go a long way in establishing a positive rapport.

Trust is the cornerstone of any successful sales relationship. To earn the trust of your customers, it is crucial to be transparent and honest. Avoid making false promises or exaggerating the benefits of your product or service. Instead, focus on providing accurate and reliable information. If you don't have an answer to a question, admit it and commit to finding the information promptly.

Consistency is another crucial factor in building trust. Follow through on your commitments and deliver on your promises. Be reliable and punctual in your interactions. By consistently meeting or exceeding expectations, you will gain the trust and confidence of your prospects.

Lastly, always prioritize the long-term relationship over short-term gains. Building trust takes time and effort, and fostering a relationship built on honesty and integrity is essential. Be patient and persistent in your approach, and remember that trust is earned over time.

In conclusion, building rapport and trust is fundamental for DSAs. You can establish a strong rapport with potential customers by approaching interactions with authenticity, finding common ground, and being transparent. You can earn their trust by consistently delivering on your promises and prioritizing the long-term relationship. Building trust is an ongoing process that requires dedication and effort, but the rewards are well worth it.

Overcoming Objections

In the world of sales, objections are bound to come up. Whether you are selling a product, service, or opportunity, you must be prepared for potential objections from your prospects. Overcoming objections is a crucial skill every

DSA must possess to succeed.

1. Understand the Objections: The first step in overcoming objections is understanding them. Take the time to listen to your prospects and identify their specific objections. Is it a financial concern? Are they unsure about the product's value? By understanding their objections, you can address them directly and provide the necessary information to alleviate their concerns.

2. Be Prepared: Anticipate common objections that may arise during the sales process. Whether it is price, quality, or competition, be ready with well-rehearsed responses highlighting your product's or service's benefits and value. This preparation will give you the confidence to handle objections effectively.

3. Active Listening: When faced with an objection, practice active listening. Allow your prospects to fully express their concerns and notice their verbal and non-verbal cues. This will show that you value their opinion and help you tailor your responses to address their specific objections.

4. Provide Solutions: Once you have identified the objections, it is essential to provide solutions. Highlight your product or service's unique features and benefits that directly address their concerns. Offer alternatives, discounts, or payment plans to overcome financial objections. The key is to provide viable solutions that demonstrate the value of what you are offering.

5. Build Trust: Overcoming objections is not just about providing solutions but also about building trust. Show empathy, be transparent, and provide honest answers to their concerns. Establishing trust will help your prospects feel more confident in buying from you.

6. Practice, Practice, Practice: Overcoming objections is a skill that improves with practice. Role-play common objections with a colleague or mentor to refine your responses and gain confidence in handling objections effectively.

The more you practice, the more natural and effortless it will become.

In conclusion, overcoming objections is an essential skill for DSAs. By understanding objections, being prepared, actively listening, providing solutions, building trust, and practicing, you can effectively address objections and close more sales. Remember, objections are not roadblocks but rather opportunities to showcase the value of your product or service. Mastering overcoming objections will set you apart from your competition and help you conquer the sales game.

Closing the Sale

Closing the sale is the pinnacle of success for DSAs. It is the moment when all the hard work and effort put into building relationships, identifying needs, and presenting solutions culminate into a successful transaction. This subchapter will delve into the art and science of closing the sale and providing expert training for DSAs in various niches.

The first step towards closing a sale is establishing trust and rapport with your potential customer. Building a relationship based on open communication and genuine interest in their needs and concerns will lay the foundation for a successful close. By actively listening and empathizing with your customer, you can understand their pain points and tailor your pitch accordingly.

Once you have identified their needs, it is time to present your solution. This is where your expertise and knowledge of your product or service come into play. Present the benefits and unique selling points clearly and concisely, highlighting how it can address their specific challenges. Use case studies, testimonials, and demonstrations to solidify their confidence in your offering further.

At this stage, objections may arise. DSAs must be prepared to handle objections effectively and turn them into opportunities. Address each objection with empathy, providing logical and persuasive counterarguments. Anticipate objections beforehand and have well-crafted responses ready to alleviate any concerns.

Timing is crucial when it comes to closing the sale. DSAs should be able to recognize buying signals and seize the right moment to ask for the sale. Use trial closes throughout the conversation to gauge the customer's interest and readiness to commit. Once you sense their enthusiasm, confidently ask for their business, using a closing technique that aligns with their personality and communication style.

1. Direct and Assertive Personality

- Technique: Clearly summarize the key points and confidently ask for commitment.
    - Example: "Based on our discussion, it seems like this solution aligns with your needs. Can we move forward with this plan?"

2. Analytical and Detail-Oriented Personality

- Technique: Provide additional data or details to reinforce the decision.
    - Example: "I've gathered additional data supporting our choice. Would you like me to share it before we finalize our decision?"

3. Expressive and Enthusiastic Personality

- Technique: Appeal to their excitement and emotion.
    - Example: "I can feel the energy about this idea! Let's seize this opportunity and make it happen. Are you on board with moving forward?"

4. Amiable and Relationship-Focused Personality

- Technique: Emphasize the positive impact on relationships.
    - Example: "Choosing this option will strengthen our collaboration and benefit our relationship. What are your thoughts on making this decision together?"

5. Assertive and Goal-Oriented Personality

- Technique: Connect the decision to achieving their goals.
    - Example: "Opting for this approach aligns perfectly with your goals. How do you see this decision contributing to achieving your objectives?"

6. Reserved and Thoughtful Personality

- Technique: Allow time for reflection and reassure them of the decision's soundness.
    - Example: "I understand you may want to think it over. Take your time, and if you have any concerns, let's discuss them. Does that sound good to you?"

Remember, the key is to adapt your closing technique to the specific characteristics of the person you're dealing with. Please pay attention to their cues, listen actively, and tailor your approach accordingly.

However, closing the sale does not mark the end of the process. Follow-up and post-sale support are equally important. DSAs should ensure customer satisfaction by providing exceptional after-sales service, addressing any concerns promptly, and maintaining open lines of communication. This fosters customer loyalty and leads to potential referrals and future sales.

Closing the sale is an art that requires constant practice and refinement. DSAs can elevate their sales game and achieve consistent success by mastering the techniques and strategies outlined in this subchapter. Remember, closing the sale is not just about making a transaction but about building lasting relationships and becoming a trusted advisor in your niche.

6

Enhancing Sales Skills

Effective Negotiation Strategies

Negotiation is a crucial skill in direct sales. As a DSA, your ability to negotiate effectively can make or break a deal. To help you conquer the sales game, this subchapter presents a range of proven negotiation strategies that will empower you to close more sales and achieve your sales targets.

1. Preparation is vital: Before entering any negotiation, it is essential to prepare thoroughly. Research the client's needs, understand their pain points, and identify their objectives. This knowledge allows you to tailor your negotiation strategy to address their requirements and offer compelling solutions.

2. Aim for a win-win outcome: Successful negotiations should not be a one-sided victory. Instead, strive for a win-win outcome where both parties feel satisfied. By focusing on creating mutual value, you build trust and establish long-term relationships, which can lead to repeat business and referrals.

3. Active listening: Listening is an art that enhances your negotiation skills. Pay close attention to the client's words, tone, and body language. You can uncover hidden insights and understand their underlying motivations by actively listening. This information is invaluable in structuring your negotiation approach and presenting tailored solutions.

4. Highlight unique selling propositions: During negotiations, emphasize your product or service's unique propositions (USPs). Clearly articulate how your offering stands out from competitors and how it directly addresses the client's pain points. Demonstrating the value and benefits of your solution will strengthen your bargaining power.

5. Be confident but flexible: Confidence is crucial in negotiations, instilling trust and credibility. However, it is equally important to remain flexible and open to compromise. Rigidity can hinder progress and result in missed opportunities. Adapt your approach to meet the client's needs while aiming to achieve your objectives.

6. Know your limits: While flexibility is crucial, it is equally important to have clear boundaries and know your limits. Understand the minimum requirements for a deal to be worthwhile for your business. This knowledge will prevent you from making detrimental concessions to your success and help maintain the profitability of your sales.

7. Seek a positive resolution: Negotiations may encounter hurdles and disagreements. However, always strive to maintain a positive and collaborative attitude. By focusing on finding resolutions rather than dwelling on conflicts, you can foster a productive negotiation environment and increase the likelihood of reaching a mutually beneficial agreement.

Remember, effective negotiation is a skill that can be learned and refined. By implementing these strategies and continuously honing your negotiation abilities, you will become a formidable force in the sales game, consistently closing deals and surpassing your targets.

Upselling and Cross-Selling Techniques

In the competitive world of sales, it is essential for DSAs to close deals and maximize their revenue potential. This subchapter discusses "Upselling and Cross-Selling Techniques" and practical strategies to help DSAs enhance their sales game and increase their profits.

Upselling refers to persuading customers to purchase a higher-priced or more advanced version of a product or service. It involves understanding customers' needs and preferences and offering them additional value options. By upselling, DSAs can increase their sales and enhance customer satisfaction by offering a more tailored solution.

One of the fundamental techniques for successful upselling is practical product knowledge. DSAs should deeply understand their product or service, including its features, benefits, and competitive advantages. This knowledge will allow them to identify opportunities for upselling and make compelling customer recommendations.

Conversely, cross-selling involves offering complementary products or services to customers who have already purchased. It is a valuable technique for increasing the average order value and expanding customer experience. By analyzing the customer's needs and preferences, DSAs can suggest additional products that enhance the value of their initial purchase.

To excel at cross-selling, DSAs should adopt a consultative approach. They should actively listen to the customer, understand their requirements, and recommend relevant products or services that align with their needs. Building rapport and trust with the customer is crucial in ensuring the success of cross-selling efforts.

Moreover, utilizing technology and data analytics can significantly enhance the effectiveness of upselling and cross-selling techniques. DSAs should leverage customer relationship management (CRM) systems and other tools to track customer preferences, purchase history, and patterns. This data can provide valuable insights for identifying upselling and cross-selling opportunities, enabling DSAs to make targeted and personalized recommendations.

In conclusion, upselling and cross-selling are valuable skills for DSAs looking to maximize their sales potential. By employing effective techniques, such as product knowledge, consultative selling, and leveraging technology, DSAs can enhance customer satisfaction, increase revenue, and excel in competitive sales.

Developing Referral Networks

In the fast-paced world of direct sales, building a solid network of referrals is vital to your success. Referrals bring in new leads and have a built-in level of trust and credibility that can significantly accelerate your sales process. This subchapter will explore the strategies and techniques you can use to develop and leverage referral networks for maximum sales impact.

1. The Power of Referrals

Referrals are like gold in the sales industry. They are warm leads that have been prequalified and come with a recommendation from someone the prospect trusts. This built-in trust can significantly reduce the time and effort required to close a deal. We will discuss the importance of referrals and why they should be a cornerstone of your sales strategy.

2. Building Relationships

Developing a solid referral network starts with building genuine relationships. We will delve into the art of relationship-building and provide practical tips on connecting with clients, colleagues, and industry influencers. By nurturing these relationships, you can position yourself as a trusted advisor and increase the likelihood of receiving valuable referrals.

3. Asking for Referrals

The key to receiving referrals is simply asking for them. We will discuss practical ways to approach clients and ask for referrals without appearing pushy or desperate. From timing your request to providing incentives, we will provide you with actionable techniques to maximize your referral acquisition.

4. Leveraging Social Media

Social media platforms have become powerful tools for developing referral networks. We will explore social media strategies, including engaging content, joining relevant groups, and utilizing LinkedIn connections. By leveraging social media effectively, you can expand your reach and tap into a vast network of potential referral sources.

5. Maintaining and Rewarding Referral Partners

Once you have established referral partnerships, it is crucial to maintain and reward them appropriately. We will discuss strategies for nurturing these relationships, such as providing ongoing support, offering incentives, and showing gratitude for successful referrals. Investing in your referral partners can create a mutually beneficial network that generates new leads.

In conclusion, developing referral networks is an essential skill for DSAs. By implementing the strategies and techniques outlined in this subchapter, you can harness the power of referrals to accelerate your sales game. Remember, building strong relationships, asking for referrals, leveraging social media, and maintaining referral partnerships are the keys to unlocking a vast network of warm leads and achieving sales success.

7

Managing Customer Relationships

Providing Excellent Customer Service

I n the competitive world of direct sales, one key factor that sets successful agents apart is their ability to provide excellent customer service. When clients feel valued and appreciated, they are likelier to become loyal customers and refer your services to others. In this subchapter, we will explore the importance of exceptional customer service and provide practical strategies for delivering it consistently.

First, DSAS must understand the significance of building strong client relationships. By listening attentively to their needs and concerns, agents can understand what their customers truly desire. This understanding enables agents to tailor their approach and provide personalized solutions, resulting in higher customer satisfaction.

One effective strategy for providing excellent customer service is to go the extra mile. This means surpassing customer expectations by offering additional assistance, providing timely follow-ups, and ensuring a smooth and seamless buying experience. By doing so, agents can create a positive impression, leaving customers with lasting trust and loyalty.

Moreover, DSAs should always strive to address customer issues or concerns proactively. Timely and efficient problem-solving is instrumental in preventing minor issues from escalating into major problems. By being proactive, agents can demonstrate their commitment to customer satisfaction and reinforce their reputation as reliable and trustworthy professionals.

Another valuable aspect of exceptional customer service is effective communication. Agents should strive to be clear, concise, and transparent in client interactions. This involves actively listening, asking pertinent questions, and providing accurate information. Agents can instill confidence and foster long-term relationships by ensuring that customers are well-informed.

Lastly, ongoing training and self-improvement are vital in providing excellent customer service. The sales field constantly evolves, and agents must stay up-to-date with industry trends and techniques. By investing in continuous learning, agents can refine their skills, adapt to changing customer expectations, and consistently deliver exceptional service.

In conclusion, providing excellent customer service is a fundamental aspect of success for DSAs. By building solid relationships, going the extra mile, being proactive, communicating effectively, and investing in continuous improvement, agents can ensure their customers receive the outstanding service they deserve. Ultimately, this commitment to excellence will drive sales and cultivate a loyal customer base that can become a powerful source of referrals and recommendations.

Handling Difficult Customers

In the fast-paced sales world, DSAs often encounter challenging customers who can test their patience and skills. Dealing with demanding customers is an art that every sales agent must master to succeed in their profession. This subchapter will give you the strategies and techniques to handle difficult customers effectively.

1. Stay Calm and Composed: When faced with a demanding customer, it's crucial to maintain your composure. Please take a deep breath and remind yourself that their behavior is not personal. Remember, you are the professional in this situation, and your calmness will help diffuse the tension.

2. Listen Actively: Difficult customers often have valid concerns or grievances. By actively listening to their needs and frustrations, you can show empathy and better understand their perspective. This step is crucial in finding a solution that satisfies both parties.

3. Empathize and Validate: Let the customer know you understand their frustration or dissatisfaction. Empathizing with their situation will help you build rapport and establish trust. Validating their emotions shows that you genuinely care about resolving the issue.

4. Offer Solutions: Once you have listened and empathized, it's time to provide solutions. Offer options that address the customer's concerns while aligning with your company's policies. Present these options clearly and concisely, ensuring the customer understands the benefits and consequences of each choice.

5. Remain Professional: Always maintain a professional demeanor no matter how difficult the customer becomes. Avoid engaging in heated arguments or taking their comments personally. Instead, find a resolution that meets their

needs and satisfies your company's policies.

6. Seek Support and Feedback: If you are unsure how to handle a demanding customer, don't hesitate to contact your supervisor or colleagues for guidance. They may have faced similar situations and can offer valuable advice based on their experience. Additionally, seek feedback from these individuals to improve your handling of challenging customers.

Remember, handling demanding customers is essential to your role as a DSA. By mastering the art of managing challenging situations, you can build stronger customer relationships, enhance your reputation, and ultimately achieve more tremendous sales success.

Building Long-Term Customer Loyalty

Building long-term customer loyalty in direct sales is not just about making a sale or meeting a quota. It is about creating lasting customer relationships that go beyond a single transaction. By building customer loyalty, you can foster a loyal customer base that will continue to support your business and become advocates for your products or services. This subchapter will explore practical strategies to help DSAs build long-term customer loyalty.

1. Understand Your Customers: To build customer loyalty, it is essential to understand your customers' needs, preferences, and pain points. Take the time to listen actively to your customers, ask open-ended questions, and gather feedback. This information will empower you to tailor your approach and offer personalized solutions that meet their requirements.

2. Provide Exceptional Customer Service: Excellent customer service is the foundation of building long-term loyalty. Ensure your customers feel valued by promptly addressing their concerns, responding, and exceeding their

expectations. Small gestures, such as handwritten thank-you notes or follow-up calls, can significantly impact customer loyalty.

3. Build Trust and Credibility: Trust is the cornerstone of any successful business relationship. Be transparent, honest, and reliable in your interactions with customers. Take the time to educate them about your products or services, providing them with accurate information to make informed decisions. Building trust and credibility will create a loyal customer base that will turn to you for their future needs.

4. Offer Ongoing Support and Education: Customer loyalty is not just about the initial sale; it requires ongoing support and education. Provide resources like newsletters, blog posts, or webinars that empower your customers to get the most out of their purchases. Be proactive in offering assistance, answering questions, and addressing any concerns.

5. Reward Loyalty: Show appreciation for your customers' loyalty by creating a rewards program or offering exclusive discounts or promotions. Rewarding their commitment strengthens their loyalty and encourages repeat purchases and referrals.

Building long-term customer loyalty is a continuous process that requires dedication, consistency, and genuine care for your customers. Implementing the strategies outlined in this subchapter will increase customer loyalty and enhance your reputation as a trusted DSA within your niche. Remember, customer loyalty is not just a one-time sale; it is an investment in the future success of your business.

8

Leveraging Technology in Sales

Utilizing CRM Systems

Managing customer relationships is crucial for DSAs in today's competitive sales landscape. This is where customer relationship management (CRM) systems come into play. A CRM system is a powerful tool that helps streamline sales processes, enhance customer interactions, and boost overall sales performance. This subchapter will explore the benefits of utilizing CRM systems and provide practical tips for DSAs to leverage these systems effectively.

One critical advantage of CRM systems is their ability to centralize customer information. By storing customer data such as contact details, purchase history, and preferences in a single, easily accessible location, DSAs can gain a comprehensive view of their customers. This allows them to personalize their sales approach, tailor their offerings to meet individual needs and build stronger relationships with their clients. With a CRM system, agents can track customer interactions, log essential notes, and set reminders, ensuring no follow-up or opportunity is missed.

CRM systems also offer valuable insights through analytics and reporting features. By analyzing data such as sales trends, customer behavior, and conversion rates, DSAs can identify areas for improvement, make data-driven decisions, and optimize their sales strategies. These systems can also automate repetitive tasks, allowing agents to focus on high-value activities such as building relationships and closing deals. With CRM systems, agents can streamline their sales processes, reduce manual errors, and increase overall efficiency.

DSAs should ensure they are familiar with the system's features and functionalities to utilize CRM systems effectively. Training and onboarding sessions are essential to ensure that agents fully understand how to input and access customer data, generate reports, and leverage the system's capabilities. Additionally, agents should make it a habit to regularly update customer information and maintain accurate records to ensure the system's effectiveness.

Furthermore, DSAS need to integrate CRM systems into their daily sales routines. Agents can maximize the system's benefits and improve sales performance by consistently logging customer interactions, following up on leads, and leveraging the system's automation features. It is also crucial to regularly review and analyze the data generated by the CRM system to identify areas for improvement and adjust sales strategies accordingly.

In conclusion, CRM systems are invaluable tools for DSAs. By centralizing customer information, providing valuable insights, and automating tasks, CRM systems enable agents to enhance customer relationships, streamline sales processes, and ultimately achieve sales success. By utilizing these systems effectively and integrating them into their daily routines, DSAs can conquer the sales game and excel in their sales training niche.

Social Media Marketing for Direct Sales

In today's digital age, social media has become essential for businesses to reach and engage with their target audience. DSAs can harness the power of social media to boost their sales and grow their customer base. This subchapter will provide valuable insights and strategies for using social media effectively in direct sales, helping agents conquer the sales game.

1. Understanding the Power of Social Media:
   Social media platforms like Facebook, Instagram, and LinkedIn have billions of active users, making them an ideal platform for reaching potential customers. DSAs must grasp the immense potential of social media and how it can amplify their sales efforts.

2. Building a Strong Online Presence:
   Creating a solid and professional online presence is crucial for direct sales success. This subchapter will guide agents in optimizing their social media profiles, including professional headshots, compelling bios, and engaging content that reflects their brand and expertise.

3. Identifying and Targeting the Right Audience:
   DSAs must identify their target audience and tailor their social media marketing efforts accordingly. This subchapter will explore practical techniques for identifying and understanding their target market's needs, preferences, and demographics.

4. Crafting Engaging Content:
   Great content is the backbone of successful social media marketing. Agents will learn how to create compelling posts, videos, and graphics that captivate their audience and leave a lasting impact. This subchapter will also explore the importance of storytelling and authenticity in content creation.

5. Leveraging Different Social Media Platforms:

Different social media platforms offer unique opportunities for DSAs. This subchapter will provide insights into leveraging popular platforms like Facebook groups, Instagram stories, and LinkedIn connections.

6. Engaging with the Audience:

Building meaningful relationships with potential customers is vital in direct sales. Agents will learn to engage with their audience through comments, direct messages, and live video sessions. This subchapter will explore techniques for fostering trust, addressing concerns, and converting leads into customers.

7. Tracking and Analyzing Results

DSAs must analyze their efforts and measure their results to refine their social media marketing strategies. This subchapter will introduce agents to various analytics tools and metrics, helping them understand what works and needs improvement.

Social media marketing has revolutionized the way businesses connect with their customers. DSAs who embrace these strategies and techniques will gain a competitive edge in the sales game, reaching a wider audience and driving more sales. By harnessing the power of social media, agents can elevate their sales training and take their direct sales business to new heights.

Analyzing Sales Data for Improved Performance

An essential introduction to statistics.

In the fast-paced world of direct sales, staying ahead of the competition requires a deep understanding of your sales performance. Analyzing sales data allows you to identify areas of improvement, make informed decisions, and boost your overall sales performance. This chapter will explore the importance of analyzing sales data and provide expert tips and strategies to leverage this information for improved results.

The Power of Sales Data Analysis

Sales data analysis is vital for DSAs looking to enhance their performance. You can gain valuable insights into your sales process by analyzing key metrics such as sales volume, customer acquisition costs, conversion rates, and average order value. This data can help you identify patterns, trends, and areas where you may fall short.

Identifying Sales Opportunities

Analyzing sales data allows you to identify potential sales opportunities that might have been overlooked. By studying customer behavior, preferences, and buying patterns, you can better understand your target audience and tailor your sales approach accordingly. For instance, if you notice a spike in sales during a particular time of year or in a specific demographic, you can adjust your marketing and sales strategies to capitalize on these trends.

Pinpointing Weaknesses

Uncovering weaknesses in your sales process is crucial for improvement. By analyzing sales data, you can pinpoint areas where you may be losing potential customers or experiencing low conversion rates. This information enables you to make targeted changes, such as improving your product knowledge, refining your pitch, or providing additional training to your sales team.

Optimizing Sales Performance

Data analysis is not just about identifying weaknesses; it also helps you optimize your sales performance. You can identify your top-performing sales strategies by tracking key metrics and replicating them across your team. Additionally, analyzing data allows you to measure the effectiveness of your marketing efforts, enabling you to allocate resources to the most successful campaigns and channels.

Conclusion

Analyzing sales data is a fundamental aspect of sales training for DSAs. By harnessing the power of data analysis, you can gain valuable insights into your sales performance, identify sales opportunities, and optimize your strategies for improved results. Embrace the power of data and let it guide you toward conquering the sales game.

9

Developing a Sales Action Plan

Creating a Daily Sales Routine

I n the fast-paced world of direct sales, having a structured and efficient daily routine is crucial to achieving success. A well-designed sales routine helps you stay organized and focused, maximizing your productivity and increasing sales. This subchapter will explore creating a daily sales routine to help DSAs conquer the sales game.

The first step in creating a daily sales routine is to set clear goals. Setting specific and achievable goals gives you a clear direction and purpose for each day. These goals could relate to the number of prospecting calls, follow-ups, or meetings you aim to complete. With these goals in mind, you can prioritize your tasks and allocate your time accordingly.

Next, it is essential to establish a consistent schedule. Determine and allocate your most productive hours to your most important sales activities. For instance, if you are most energetic and focused in the mornings, reserve that time for prospecting and making sales calls. You can optimize your performance and yield better results by aligning your daily activities with your natural energy levels.

Moreover, a successful sales routine involves a combination of proactive and reactive tasks. While proactive tasks involve actively seeking new leads and reaching out to potential clients, reactive tasks involve responding to inquiries, following up with existing clients, and nurturing relationships. Balancing these two types of tasks is crucial to maintaining a steady flow of sales opportunities.

Additionally, incorporating regular self-improvement activities into your daily routine is vital for sales success. Dedicate time to reading sales books, attending webinars or seminars, and staying updated on industry trends. Continuous learning and personal development will enhance your knowledge, skills, and confidence, allowing you to become a more effective sales agent.

Lastly, it is essential to track and measure your progress. Review your daily sales activities and outcomes regularly to identify areas for improvement. Use metrics such as conversion rates, average order value, and customer satisfaction to evaluate your performance and make necessary adjustments to your routine.

In conclusion, creating an effective daily sales routine is fundamental to conquering the sales game as a DSA. By setting goals, establishing a consistent schedule, balancing proactive and reactive tasks, investing in self-improvement, and tracking progress, you can maximize your productivity, increase your sales, and ultimately achieve success in the competitive world of direct sales.

Time Management for DSAs

In the cutthroat world of sales, time is money. DSAs are constantly juggling multiple tasks, clients, and opportunities. Effectively managing your time can be the difference between soaring success and frustrating mediocrity. This subchapter will provide valuable insights and strategies to help DSAs conquer time management challenges and maximize productivity.

1. Prioritize Your Tasks: As a DSA, it's crucial to identify and prioritize your most important tasks. Determine which activities will most significantly impact your sales and focus on those first. This includes following up with leads, scheduling appointments, and delivering exceptional customer service.

2. Set Clear Goals: Goal setting is essential for any sales professional. Setting clear, specific goals allows you to align your time and efforts accordingly. Break down your goals into smaller, achievable targets, and create a roadmap to success. Regularly review and adjust your goals as necessary.

3. Plan Your Schedule: A well-structured schedule can help you stay organized and focused. Use a planner or digital calendar to map your activities, appointments, and deadlines. Set aside time for prospecting, networking, sales calls, and administrative tasks. Be sure to build in buffers for unexpected interruptions or emergencies.

4. Delegate and Outsource: Recognize that you can't do everything. Delegate tasks that others, such as administrative work, social media management, or lead generation, can handle. Outsource tasks that are not your expertise or require specialized skills. This will free up your time and allow you to focus on revenue-generating activities.

5. Master Time Blocking: Time blocking involves setting aside specific time blocks for different activities. This technique helps you stay disciplined and

focused. For example, allocate a block of time in the morning for prospecting and lead generation and another for client meetings or follow-ups in the afternoon. Avoid multitasking and commit fully to the task during each time block.

6. Avoid Time Wasters: Identify and eliminate or minimize everyday time-wasting activities. This includes excessive social media use, unnecessary meetings, or unproductive conversations. Use productivity apps or website blockers to stay focused and limit distractions.

7. Take Care of Yourself: Effective time management also involves self-care. Prioritize your physical and mental well-being by getting enough sleep, eating healthily, and exercising regularly. Take breaks throughout the day to recharge and avoid burnout.

By implementing these time management strategies, DSAs can streamline their workflow, increase productivity, and ultimately conquer the sales game. Remember, time is your most valuable asset – use it wisely, and success will follow.

Evaluating and Adjusting Strategies

In the fast-paced world of direct sales, it is crucial for sales agents to constantly evaluate and adjust their strategies to stay ahead of the game. This subchapter will provide DSAs with expert training on effectively evaluating their current strategies and making necessary adjustments to maximize their sales potential.

Evaluation is vital in the sales process as it allows sales agents to identify what is working well and what may need improvement. By analyzing their sales techniques, agents can gain valuable insights into their strengths and weaknesses, enabling them to fine-tune their approach. This subchapter will guide sales agents through various evaluation methods, including tracking key performance indicators, gathering customer feedback, and conducting self-assessments.

One of the essential evaluation tools covered in this subchapter is tracking key performance indicators (KPIs). Sales agents will learn to identify and measure KPIs specific to their sales goals, such as conversion rates, average order value, and customer acquisition costs. By regularly monitoring these metrics, agents can assess the effectiveness of their strategies and make data-driven decisions for improvement.

Another crucial aspect of evaluation is gathering customer feedback. DSAs will discover how to actively seek customer feedback to understand their needs, preferences, and pain points. By listening to their customers, agents can identify areas where their strategies may fall short and adjust accordingly.

Furthermore, this subchapter will provide sales agents with techniques for self-assessment. Self-reflection is a powerful tool for identifying personal strengths and weaknesses, enabling agents to enhance their skills continuously. Agents will learn how to evaluate their communication style, negotiation tactics, and problem-solving abilities to pinpoint areas for growth.

Once the evaluation process is complete, this subchapter will guide sales agents in making necessary adjustments to their strategies. Agents will gain insights into various adjustment techniques, such as refining their target market, updating their sales pitch, or adopting new technologies. By staying flexible and adapting to changing market dynamics, sales agents can consistently improve their performance and achieve their sales goals.

In conclusion, "Evaluating and Adjusting Strategies" is a critical subchapter in the book "*Conquer the Sales Game: Expert Training for DSAs.*" By providing DSAs with the knowledge and tools to evaluate and adjust their strategies effectively, this subchapter aims to empower sales agents to maximize their sales potential and excel in their sales field.

10

Overcoming Sales Slumps and Rejections

Maintaining Motivation During Difficult Times

Maintaining motivation during difficult times is essential for success in the fast-paced world of direct sales. As a DSA, you face numerous challenges daily - rejections, missed targets, and setbacks that can quickly dampen your spirits. However, during these challenging times, your true character as a salesperson is tested. This subchapter will provide valuable insights and strategies to help you stay motivated and conquer the sales game, even when the going gets tough.

1. Set Clear Goals: One of the most effective ways to maintain motivation is by setting clear and achievable goals. Break down your larger sales targets into smaller, more manageable milestones. This will give you a sense of progress and accomplishment, keeping you motivated to push forward.

2. Celebrate Small Wins: Remember to celebrate even minor victories. Whether you close a problematic sale or receive positive feedback from a customer, take the time to acknowledge and reward yourself for your achievements. This will provide a much-needed boost to your motivation and confidence.

3. Seek Support: Contact your colleagues and mentors during difficult times. Share your challenges and seek advice from those who have faced similar situations. Surrounding yourself with a positive and supportive network will help you stay motivated and inspired.

4. Stay Positive: Maintaining a positive mindset is crucial during challenging times. Instead of dwelling on failures or setbacks, focus on the lessons learned and the growth opportunities. Positive self-talk and visualization techniques can help you stay motivated and maintain a can-do attitude.

5. Continuous Learning: Invest in your personal and professional development by continuously learning and honing your sales skills. Attend sales training workshops, read books, and seek new strategies and techniques. The more knowledge and expertise you have, the more confident and motivated you will be.

6. Take Breaks: It's essential to give yourself regular breaks to recharge and rejuvenate. Direct sales can be demanding, both mentally and physically. Take time off to relax, indulge in hobbies, and spend quality time with loved ones. This will help you maintain a healthy work-life balance and prevent burnout.

Remember, difficult times are temporary, and maintaining motivation is crucial for long-term success in the sales game. By setting clear goals, celebrating small wins, seeking support, staying positive, continuously learning, and taking breaks, you will be able to conquer any challenge that comes your way and achieve outstanding results in your direct sales career. Stay motivated, stay focused, and keep pushing forward toward greatness.

Dealing with Rejection and Bouncing Back

In direct sales, rejection is an inevitable part of the game. No matter how skilled or experienced you are, there will always be potential customers who decline your offer. However, the key to success is handling rejection and returning more potent than ever.

First and foremost, it's crucial to develop a resilient mindset. Understand that rejection is not personal but a part of the sales process. Remind yourself that every "no" brings you one step closer to a "yes." Embrace rejection as an opportunity to learn and improve your approach. By maintaining a positive attitude, you'll be better equipped to handle setbacks and keep moving forward.

One effective strategy for dealing with rejection is to reflect on each encounter. Take the time to analyze what went wrong and identify areas for improvement. Perhaps you must refine your pitch, address objections more effectively, or enhance your product knowledge. By actively seeking feedback and learning from your experiences, you'll be able to adapt and overcome obstacles more efficiently.

Another crucial aspect is building and maintaining a solid support network. Surround yourself with like-minded individuals who understand the challenges of direct sales. Share your experiences, seek advice, and learn from others who have faced rejection and come out on top. Remember, you're not alone in this journey, and having a support system can provide you with the motivation and encouragement needed to bounce back from rejection.

Furthermore, honing your sales skills through continuous training is vital. A successful DSA never stops learning. Stay updated on industry trends, study successful sales techniques, and invest in professional development courses. By constantly sharpening your skills, you'll be better equipped to handle rejection and turn it into an opportunity for growth.

Finally, always remember to take care of yourself. Rejection can sometimes take a toll on your confidence and motivation. Engage in activities that help you relax and recharge. Whether it's exercise, meditation, or spending time with loved ones, make self-care a priority. Taking care of your mental and physical well-being will ensure you have the resilience and energy to bounce back stronger after facing rejection.

In conclusion, rejection is an integral part of the sales game. By adopting a resilient mindset, seeking feedback, building a support network, continuously learning, and prioritizing self-care, DSAs can effectively deal with rejection and bounce back, which is more vital than ever. Remember, every rejection brings you closer to success. Embrace the challenges and keep persevering towards your goals.

Strategies for Overcoming Sales Slumps

In the fast-paced and competitive world of direct sales, every sales agent will experience a sales slump at some point in their career. Sales slumps can be frustrating and demotivating, but they are opportunities for growth and self-improvement. This subchapter will provide you, DSAs, with practical strategies to overcome sales slumps and get back on track to achieving your sales goals.

1. Evaluate and Reflect: The first step in overcoming a sales slump is to evaluate your current sales strategies and performance. Reflect on what may have caused the slump—was it a change in the market, lack of motivation, or ineffective sales techniques? Identifying the root cause will help you develop a targeted plan to overcome the slump.

2. Revisit your Goals: Reconnecting with your sales goals and understanding why you are in this profession can reignite your passion and motivation. Take the time to reassess your short-term and long-term goals and break them down into smaller, achievable targets. This will help you regain focus and work towards tangible outcomes.

3. Enhance your Skills: Sales is an ever-evolving field, and ongoing training is essential for success. Use the time during a sales slump to invest in your professional development. Seek sales training programs, read books on sales techniques, or attend industry conferences and workshops. Enhancing your skills will boost your confidence and equip you with new strategies to tackle sales challenges.

4. Engage with Your Network: One of the most effective ways to overcome a sales slump is by contacting your existing network. Connect with past clients, colleagues, and friends to remind them of your services or products. Leverage the power of referrals and testimonials to increase your credibility and attract new customers. Additionally, consider joining professional networking groups or online communities to expand your network and gain new leads.

5. Focus on Relationship Building: Sales is not just about transactions; it's about building meaningful customer relationships. During a sales slump, shift your focus from the numbers to fostering genuine connections with your clients. Take the time to understand their needs, provide exceptional customer service, and go the extra mile to exceed their expectations. Building strong relationships will lead to repeat business and generate positive word-of-mouth referrals.

Remember, sales slumps are temporary setbacks that can be overcome with the right strategies and mindset. By evaluating your performance, revisiting your goals, enhancing your skills, engaging with your network, and focusing on relationship building, you will be well on your way to conquering any sales slump that comes your way. Stay motivated, persevere, and keep honing your craft as a DSA. Success is just around the corner!

11

Continuous Learning and Professional Growth

Staying Updated with Industry Trends

I n the fast-paced sales world, DSAS must stay updated with the latest industry trends. The sales landscape constantly evolves; what worked yesterday may not work today. By staying ahead of the curve and keeping abreast of industry trends, DSAs can gain a competitive edge and achieve greater success in their sales efforts.

One of the key reasons for staying updated with industry trends is to understand customers' changing needs and preferences. Agents can identify new opportunities and tailor their sales strategies by staying informed about the latest market trends. For example, suppose a particular product or service is gaining popularity among customers. In that case, agents can focus on promoting and selling that product, thereby increasing their chances of success.

Furthermore, staying updated with industry trends enables DSAs to anticipate and adapt to changes in the market. Whether it's the introduction of new technologies, shifts in consumer behavior, or emerging sales techniques, being aware of these trends allows agents to stay ahead of the competition. By embracing new ideas and incorporating them into their sales approach, agents can better position themselves as industry leaders and trusted advisors to their customers.

DSAs can utilize various resources to stay updated with industry trends. One effective method is to attend conferences, seminars, and trade shows related to the sales industry. These events provide valuable networking opportunities and insights into the latest trends and best practices. Additionally, agents can subscribe to industry publications, blogs, and newsletters to receive regular updates on market trends and sales strategies.

Another valuable resource is social media platforms, where industry thought leaders often share their insights and experiences. Agents can stay connected with the latest industry developments by following influential sales professionals, participating in relevant online communities, and engaging in meaningful discussions with peers.

In conclusion, staying updated with industry trends is essential for DSAs to thrive. By understanding customer needs, anticipating market changes, and embracing new ideas, agents can position themselves as industry leaders and achieve tremendous success in their sales efforts. By attending industry events, subscribing to publications, and leveraging social media platforms, agents can ensure they are always up to date with the latest trends and best practices in the dynamic sales world.

Attending Sales Training and Workshops

As a DSA, it is crucial to continuously develop your skills and stay updated with the latest strategies and techniques to conquer the sales game. One of the most effective ways to achieve this is by attending sales training and workshops. These events provide invaluable opportunities to enhance knowledge, learn from industry experts, and network with like-minded professionals.

Sales training and workshops offer a structured learning environment where you can gain insights into various aspects of the sales process. Whether you are a seasoned salesperson or new to the field, these sessions cater to individuals at all levels of expertise. From prospecting and lead generation to closing deals and maintaining customer relationships, you will find workshops that cover every aspect of the sales cycle.

By participating in sales training and workshops, you learn from experienced sales trainers who have achieved remarkable success in the industry. They will share their tried and tested strategies, tips, and techniques that have helped them excel in their careers. You will gain a deep understanding of consumer psychology, practical communication skills, and negotiation tactics that you can apply to your sales approach.

Networking opportunities at these events are also invaluable. You will have the chance to meet fellow sales agents from different niches, exchange ideas, and build relationships that may lead to collaborative partnerships or mentorship opportunities. The sales industry is constantly evolving, and by connecting with other professionals, you can stay updated with the latest trends and best practices.

Attending sales training and workshops demonstrates your commitment to professional growth and development. It shows your employers and clients that you are dedicated to honing your skills and providing the best possible service. This can increase credibility, trust and higher sales conversions.

To make the most out of sales training and workshops, it is important to approach them with an open mind and a willingness to learn. Take notes, ask questions, and actively participate in group activities. Implement the knowledge and techniques you acquire into your daily sales routine, and continually evaluate and refine your strategies based on the insights gained from these events.

In conclusion, attending sales training and workshops is vital to your professional development as a DSA. The knowledge, skills, and connections you gain from these experiences will empower you to conquer the sales game and achieve your goals. So, take advantage of these opportunities, stay ahead of the competition, and elevate your sales career to new heights.

Networking with Other Sales Professionals

In competitive sales, networking with other professionals is crucial to success. Connecting with other sales agents can enhance your knowledge, give you valuable insights, and create mutually beneficial relationships. This sub-chapter explores the importance of networking and provides practical tips on effectively connecting with other sales professionals.

Why Networking Matters

Networking allows you to tap into the knowledge and experience of others in your field. By building relationships with fellow sales agents, you can learn from their successes and failures, expanding your skillset and improving your sales techniques. Networking also provides a platform for sharing ideas, strategies, and best practices, leading to personal and professional growth.

How to Network Effectively

1. Attend industry conferences and events: These gatherings offer ample opportunities to meet and connect with other sales professionals. Engage in conversations, exchange business cards, and follow up with potential connections after the event.

2. Join professional organizations: Sales training associations and industry-specific groups provide a platform for networking and learning from seasoned sales professionals. Attend meetings, participate in discussions, and take advantage of educational resources offered by these organizations.

3. Utilize social media: Platforms like LinkedIn and Twitter offer virtual networking opportunities. Connect with other sales agents, join relevant groups, and engage in discussions to expand your network and stay updated on industry trends.

4. Seek mentorship: Forming a mentor-mentee relationship with an experienced sales professional can accelerate your growth. Look for someone who inspires you and is willing to share their knowledge and expertise.

5. Create a referral network: Collaborating with other sales agents to refer potential clients to one another can be a win-win situation. Building a network of trusted professionals can expand your reach and increase your chances of closing more deals.

Benefits of Networking

1. Learning and growth: Networking exposes you to different perspectives, ideas, and strategies that can enhance your sales skills and knowledge.

2. Support system: Connecting with other sales professionals provides a support system where you can share challenges, seek advice, and find

encouragement during difficult times.

3. Collaboration opportunities: Networking can lead to partnerships or collaborative projects benefiting both parties.

4. Access to new opportunities: Through networking, you can gain knowledge about job openings, potential clients, and industry events that may not be publicly advertised.

Remember, successful networking is about what you can gain and how you can contribute. Be genuine, build relationships based on trust and mutual respect, and always be willing to offer support and assistance to your fellow sales professionals.

In conclusion, networking with other sales professionals is essential to sales training. By actively engaging in networking activities, you can enhance your skills, gain new insights, and create a robust support system within the industry. Embrace networking as a valuable tool for professional growth and success in the competitive sales arena.

12

Achieving Long-term Success in Direct Sales

Setting New Goals and Targets

One critical ingredient for success in the sales game is the ability to set new goals and targets. As DSAs, we must constantly challenge ourselves and strive for improvement.

This subchapter will delve into the importance of setting new goals and targets for DSAs and provide expert training to help you conquer the sales game.

In the dynamic world of sales, stagnation is not an option. Setting new goals and targets helps to keep us motivated and focused on our objectives. It allows us to push beyond our comfort zones and reach new heights of success. By constantly setting new goals, we can elevate our performance and achieve outstanding results.

The first step in setting new goals and targets is reflecting on your achievements. Take the time to review your sales performance and identify areas where you have excelled and areas where improvement is needed. This self-assessment will help you identify your strengths and weaknesses, enabling you to set realistic and attainable goals.

Once you have assessed your performance, it is time to set specific, measurable, achievable, relevant, and time-bound (SMART) goals. SMART goals are essential in providing clarity and focus. They serve as a roadmap to guide your actions and measure your progress. Whether it is increasing your sales volume, expanding your customer base, or enhancing your product knowledge, SMART goals will help you stay on track and ensure your efforts are aligned with your objectives.

Breaking down new goals and targets into smaller, actionable steps is essential for effectively setting them. This approach will also help you track your progress and celebrate small victories, keeping you from feeling overwhelmed and motivated throughout the journey.

In addition to setting goals, it is crucial to establish a system for monitoring and evaluating your progress. Review your goals and targets regularly to ensure you are on the right path. Adjust your strategies and tactics to align with your objectives if necessary.

Remember, setting new goals and targets is not a one-time event. It is an ongoing process that requires dedication and commitment. You will conquer the sales game and achieve unparalleled success as a DSA by continuously challenging yourself and striving for improvement.

In conclusion, setting new goals and targets is essential for DSAs. You can elevate your performance and conquer the sales game by reflecting on past achievements, setting SMART goals, breaking them down into actionable steps, and regularly monitoring progress. Embrace the power of goal setting and embark on a journey of continuous growth and success in direct sales.

Becoming a Leader in the Field

In the fast-paced world of direct sales, being a leader in the field is crucial for success. As a DSA, you have the opportunity to not only achieve your own financial goals but also to inspire and guide others in their own sales journey. This subchapter will provide you with valuable insights and strategies to help you become a true leader in the field of direct sales.

First and foremost, leadership starts with personal development. Investing in yourself continuously and your skills is crucial to stay ahead of the game. This means seeking sales training programs, attending workshops, and reading books on sales techniques and strategies. By constantly improving your knowledge and skills, you will become a trusted authority in your field and be able to provide valuable guidance to your team.

Leading by example is another critical aspect of becoming a leader in the field. Your actions speak louder than words, and your team will look up to you for guidance and inspiration. Show them what it takes to succeed by consistently achieving your sales targets and demonstrating a solid work ethic. This will motivate your team to follow in your footsteps and strive for excellence.

Effective communication is also vital to being a successful leader. Regularly communicate with your team, providing them with valuable feedback and support. Be available to answer their questions, address their concerns, and provide guidance when needed. By fostering open and transparent communication, you will build trust and loyalty within your team, which is essential for long-term success.

In addition to personal development, leading by example, and effective communication, creating a positive and empowering team culture is crucial. Foster a supportive environment where team members feel valued and encouraged to grow. Recognize and celebrate their achievements and provide opportunities for them to develop their leadership skills. By investing in the growth and success of your team members, you will create a solid and cohesive team that will drive results.

Becoming a leader in the field of direct sales takes time and effort, but the rewards are well worth it. By continuously developing yourself, leading by example, communicating effectively, and fostering a positive team culture, you will achieve your own goals and inspire and guide others to reach their full potential in direct sales.

Celebrating Achievements and Reflecting on Growth

In the fast-paced world of direct sales, sales agents must take a moment to celebrate their achievements and reflect on their growth. This subchapter emphasizes the importance of acknowledging successes and learning from experiences in the field of direct sales. By doing so, sales agents can boost their motivation and confidence, enhance their overall performance, and pave the way for continuous improvement.

One of the most effective ways to celebrate achievements is by setting goals and milestones. DSAs should establish clear objectives, whether reaching a particular sales target, acquiring a specific number of new clients, or mastering a particular sales technique. When these goals are accomplished, it is essential to acknowledge and celebrate them. This can be done through small rewards or recognition within the sales team, fostering a positive and encouraging environment that fuels further success.

Equally important is the practice of reflecting on growth. DSAs should regularly evaluate their performance and analyze their successes and failures. By reflecting on what worked and what didn't, agents can identify areas for improvement and make necessary adjustments to their sales strategies. This self-reflection process allows for personal and professional growth, enabling sales agents to become more effective and efficient.

Moreover, celebrating achievements and reflecting on growth should not be limited to individual efforts. Team celebrations and reflections play a vital role in sales training. Encouraging team members to share their successes and challenges fosters a collective learning environment where agents can benefit from each other's experiences. Celebrating team achievements boosts morale and promotes a sense of unity, enhancing collaboration and cooperation among team members.

In conclusion, celebrating achievements and reflecting on growth is integral to the direct sales journey. By setting goals, celebrating milestones, and engaging in self-reflection, sales agents can fuel their motivation, enhance their performance, and foster a culture of continuous improvement. Moreover, team celebrations and reflections provide a supportive and collaborative sales training environment. Ultimately, embracing this practice will empower DSAs to conquer the sales game and achieve lasting career success.

Conclusion: Conquering the Sales Game as a DSA

Congratulations, DSAs, on completing this comprehensive training program to help you conquer the sales game! Throughout this book, we have explored various strategies, techniques, and skills essential for your success in the competitive world of direct sales. With this knowledge, you can take your sales game to new heights.

In today's fast-paced and ever-evolving marketplace, being a successful DSA requires more than just a charming personality and a persuasive pitch. It demands a deep understanding of your product or service, practical communication skills, and a relentless drive to achieve your sales goals. You can position yourself as a top-performing sales agent in your niche by mastering these essential elements.

One of the key takeaways from this book is the importance of building solid relationships with your customers. As a DSA, you can interact directly with your potential clients, allowing you to connect with them. By genuinely understanding their needs, concerns, and desires, you can tailor your sales approach to provide the best solutions and exceed their expectations.

Another crucial aspect of conquering the sales game is continuous learning and self-improvement. The sales landscape constantly changes, and staying ahead of the curve is vital. Embrace opportunities for professional development, attend workshops, and seek mentorship from seasoned sales professionals. Adopt a growth mindset and be open to adapting your strategies as you encounter new challenges or market trends.

Additionally, always remember the power of persistence and resilience. Sales can be a brutal and sometimes demoralizing profession; however, by maintaining a positive mindset and bouncing back from setbacks, you can overcome any obstacles that come your way. Celebrate your wins, learn from your losses, and never lose sight of your ultimate sales goals.

As you embark on your journey as a DSA, remember that success is not measured solely by the number of sales you make but also by the relationships you build, the value you provide to your customers, and the satisfaction you derive from your work. Stay passionate, stay motivated, and always strive for excellence.

In conclusion, applying the strategies and techniques discussed in this book gives you the tools to conquer the sales game as a DSA. You can achieve unparalleled success in your sales career with persistence, continuous learning, and a customer-centric approach. Now, go out there and make a lasting impact with your sales prowess!

Remember, you are not just a sales agent but a sales game-changer!

About the Author

Enrique D. Trujillo, a native of Bogota, Colombia, embarked on a transformative journey that led him from the vibrant streets of South America to the corridors of academic achievement and professional success in the United States.

Enrique's early academic pursuits took him to a Veterinary College in Colombia, where he honed his dedication and discipline. In 1979, driven by a thirst for knowledge and new experiences, he crossed borders to pursue higher education in the United States. His academic endeavors led him to the University of Wisconsin-Milwaukee, where he earned a Bachelor of Science in Microbiology, a testament to his commitment to intellectual growth and academic excellence.

The pursuit of education was not without its challenges, and Enrique's entrepreneurial spirit emerged as he found innovative ways to fund his college journey. Summers were transformed into opportunities for personal and professional development as he undertook the role of a door-to-door book salesman with The Southwestern Publishing Company in Nashville, TN. This experience provided financial support and valuable skills shaping Enrique's future endeavors.

Enrique's ability to lead and inspire others became evident during his involvement with The Southwestern Program. His outstanding contributions were recognized with the prestigious President Recommendation Award for recruiting ten students for door-to-door sales for the summer. His continued dedication led to an Honorary Bachelor of Sales and Business Management degree for successfully recruiting a second 13-member team in his third summer—an accomplishment that foreshadowed his future leadership in the business world.

Embracing the world of finance, Enrique joined the bank card industry, where his commitment to excellence propelled him to the top, achieving the rank of number 1 office out of 100 in the United States. Fueled by a vision for personal and professional growth, he took the entrepreneurial leap, establishing his own company—a testament to his resilience, leadership, and strategic acumen.

Enrique's latest venture involves sharing his wealth of knowledge and experience with others through his book, "*Conquer the Sales Game.*" This publication encapsulates the wisdom gained from years in the business world and is a vital resource in the training and coaching sessions he is developing. As a seasoned entrepreneur, mentor, and author, Enrique D. Trujillo continues to make an indelible mark on the world of business, inspiring others to conquer their own sales game and achieve unprecedented success.

You can connect with me on:
🌐 https://www.enriquetrujillo.us
f https://facebook.com/djrastamaxx

Subscribe to my newsletter:

✉ https://enriquetrujillo.substack.com

www.ingramcontent.com/pod-product-compliance
Lightning Source LLC
Chambersburg PA
CBHW071503210326
41597CB00018B/2669